MAXIMS FROM MY MOTHER'S MILK
HYMNS TO HIM   A DIALOGUE

2/2002

Also by Douglas Messerli

River to Rivet: A Poetic Trilogy
    Dinner on the Lawn (1979, 1982)
    River to Rivet: A Manifesto (1984)
    Some Distance (1982)
Contemporary American Fiction [ed. with an introduction] (1983)
"Language" Poetries: An Anthology [ed. with an
    introduction] (1987)

Maxims from My Mother's Milk
Hymns to Him

A Dialogue
By Douglas Messerli

 Sun & Moon Press
Los Angeles

© 1988 by Douglas Messerli
Cover: *Untitled*, by Jan Knap; permission to reprint from Paul
Maenz Gallery, Köln and Holly Solomon Gallery,
New York.

Some of the poems of this collection have previously
appeared in the magazines *Aerial*, *boundary 2* ["43 Poets
(1984)", ed. by Charles Bernstein], *Conjunctions*, *Frank*
[France], *The Legionnaire*, *Notus*, *Southpaw*, and *Temblor*.

Library of Congress Cataloging in Publication Data

Messerli, Douglas
　　　　Maxims from my mother's milk/hymns to him:
　　　　A dialogue

I. Title

ISBN: 1-55713-047-7
ISBN: 2-55713-013-0

5　　4　　3　　2　　1

Sun & Moon Press
6148 Wilshire Boulevard
Gertrude Stein Plaza
Los Angeles, California
(213) 857-1115

for my parents
John and Lorna

Now the maxim is comprised in an essentialist notion of human nature, it is linked to classical ideology: it is the most arrogant (often the stupidest) of the forms of language. Why then not reject it? The reason is, as always, emotive: I write maxims (or I sketch their movement) in order to reassure myself: *when some disturbance arises, I attenuate it by confiding myself to a fixity which exceeds my powers:* "Actually, it's always like that": *and the maxim is born. The maxim is a sort of* sentence-name, *and to name is to pacify. Moreover, this too is a maxim: it attenuates my fear of seeking extravagance by writing maxims.*

—*Roland Barthes*, Roland Barthes

*Sing hymns to God in <u>his</u> house
Not at home to your spouse.
—Popular rhyme*

TABLE OF CONTENTS

Sometimes a sentence ends in imprisonment.

PANDORA'S BOX

Start and you have . . . a jar to leave open
that can release whatever was
within, there's nothing that's all

and everything that's not
's tied round the neck
as smack drives a buss
into the mouth of another

gap where knees come together
waiting for the weight
of whatever might
be strong enough to hang
from that hope.

GETTING STARTED

Out of words / come the mouths of babes
bursting into long—————
abort of it.

Out of the addled / gently knocking
the heir—————
falls

on bereft ears. / The line should be
weaned —————
not deferred.

You don't put off / the farrow
when you have—————
the hay!

Good lines are leans to an in.

ON THE LINE

A line is a movement into correction. The way you run
   for a bus

when you've slept beyond the clock. In this sense it
   isn't simply a stop—

you drop from the moving vehicle with a dash, a
   comma curbs the desire

to get there. Assign a period to it and you've put an end
   to destination.

In short there is a purpose to punctuation that's seldom
   grounded

in grammar.

WATCH

the horizon stretches—suddenly out

of nowhere

a swimmer

sleeping on

the sand rises up

nakedly

to wave

his trunks

falling

into what is

between us

& land, leaving everyone impatient

ly staring

at where we are

soon to set

foot.

*To think is to place words in motion, to act is to race them to
  devotion.*

EN ROUTE (NARCISSUS)

Rising just

a little under

the weather

's cold

ing the cat

atonic man in the mirror

for making him come

from such a sweet sleep

er to sink

& revive with his hand

upon the hand

dle of the raz

or he shaves within

an inch of his life.

THE NEXT THING THAT WANTS

after Jonathan Edwards

The next Thing that Wants

to Carry the Web

away from Spider

Extends Now

into so slender

an Eternity We

Hold in our

Breathe & It's compleat—there

between the Chair

& the Prayer

in wait

of Weight.

The meter of the mind doesn't move on feet.

EAR ENDOW

I'd gladly let my foot
step into line to kick
the sit from any rhyme
defining as its end
its readers' (s)a(ti)s
factions.

THE FRANTIC LOOK

Something to unfold
from the foot
of this net, yet
falling into place ahead
of lime. Out of trees
little quail, flinch
into flee as shelled
peas into a gal-
vanized bucket. This skin's
transparent as stain
berried lips skimming
milk of human
kindness. The nose
can never,
like a lady with a fan
who won't leave her
ever.

Meaning meets at the weave of word and frays.

ALLER ET RETOUR

Write often the bat insists. It doubles its lips
and slips into something said. It can never be
natural to wing a sentence when a word might
work for instance, blink and the ball spins
into the glove.

ON EDGE

Appreciation is to precipice like
what makes the edge so
loose beneath the shoe, the rocks ready to
have, been swallowed by the gorges!
Valleys are always hungry
for the mountains, the valet waits
on the suitor. Love is like that
break between where
it emanates and is
highly regarded.

A verb should never be applied to curb.

FROM HEAR TO AIR

Poetry is always seeking something special. To men with
  leashed dogs leave

everyday life. A poem is not a window but a door through
  which anyone who opens

it must move beyond the hoed field to a dazzling
  constipation

of blindingly bright scars. "Back into the house," someone
  shouts. "Meteorites!"

Others sneak a peak through blinds calling their kitchens
  into wives.

Since conception some have stayed in bed and said "I can't
  understand

why anyone would want to go so far." The net

gain isn't absolute. Some prefer peanuts to porcupines and I
  don't

blame them but—perhaps beneath his quills the meat would
  be marvelous

to eat with dill or then again it might be tough. In any case
  there's a pocket

to keep pens in. The proposition is to sign away your life,
  to leave no terrain

untouched.

CALLS OF NATURE: A SQUARE DANCE

First cane reed!

The thistle calls
the bell to pick.

On the patter later
bear the flower
to with stand!

The bee falls in
to what it sips.

Breed it into bread!

What picks them up
plaits the peppers.

Place the necklace
after round the stem
of the carafe!

The rose rise
s to it slips.

Stop the stalk!

The stamen drops
insects into cup.

When nectar's drunk
raise a ruckus finally

doodle on a clarinet!

A pause. What pricks
the thumb surprises.

First read cane!

Etc.

MAXIMS FROM MY MOTHER'S MILK

Meaning is the mutter of intention, intention the udder of regret.

NIGHT TRAIN

for Jim Wine

The world in some sense must—break
the floe—summer breezes. the mourning
doves into its own after—coo
ling the fire
flies—& frees us.

THE ANNUNCIATION

See the world! the tussles
of the tree against
its own branches! The breeze
settles into teeth
as cavities, the fruit
in crib, the curtain
from its cornice—there!
is the patient
bed, loaded
with a coat of every guest.
The grass has been tracked
down in mud
as chins of sons become
beards of fathers, breathlessly
pausing to protect some would
be mother.

      She on her part
has rested the plate
upon tectonics—slightly
terrified of tremors *he*
hasn't heard yet. On the one hand

23

there's the knife raised
to cut china, on the other
there's a pat
turn projected on the back
of the agitated
girl, the sun
shining through the caught
drape. Drop it!

The word dictates its meaning to append.

DECLINE AND FALL

The word seldom can collapse. Consider the collapse, how
  its extremities predict

the act. When we Calypso the mind creates a floor on which
  to dance.

But what if the word never was said? Must the marathoners be
  carried

off? Even the good judge of character might fear that in wiping
  his slate

clear he may erase the steps for the survival of the race.
  Nothing is always

something that is not. And this hangs a cross from his throat.

That's the paradox, that a neck is the perfect place for the
  embrace

of the rope. Perhaps that's why they hung *Il Duce* from his feet
  at the fall

of the Fascists.

A VECTOR OF THE STRADDLE

after John Donne

Sandhill & lye still need the sea.
Conjecture, dove, above theosophy.
    Trees, the flower at bee, salve scent
    Stalking dear through meadow's dent
A song, mythos: hitched knee, lower calves seduced
Put low the one his lust loved t'ward bed.
    (See—through clothes addle thread).
    Man to save Eros falls, sings arias to soothe
Though guiles sour & pant above his bow.
The skies have hid, land rattles, grows
Dumb, blustering, tears; glut rots blisses' grotto.

Fat plovers at the rotted grain fly free
O'er ditches, rills indigent, best mothers be.

A lie's at the heart of every lay.

LULLABY

Some thing falls into in
finity. what lie
can be stood, on its head
the old mattress spring
s into action, singing of course
I've no hard rocks—
but at least it beats
having to sleep
on what the mind conjures
up from crevices of beautiful
black—wacke!

SWAN DIVE

> *Was what was good for Zeus*
> *Good for a gander?*
>
> (Children's riddle)

proceeding neither nor
                   ahead aimlessly sets
                                    the shore
sure
the very blow
               would steep

down and begin becoming
decent? sound
               expects
               a cadence caught
                              up marshes
thi–
s way—

stuck thumb!

        reaches down

        for above

               what folds

in a curve

of bentage

       livéd in the lost, arms

                 spread

                     ing in bare

bushes where gardens have been

               cut squat

               & squared

                   to rise of both

                   climber and rose

he leaves

a corn

—er to oak

There!
where he lay
her skin, white as Sodomites

come down
to a tale

at this point
she spoke:

You make me feel

dirty and tired

and old.

In a tale it's impossible that anything's ahead.

WAITING FOR THE BALLAD TO BEGIN

Halt sings into lapse
to further the after
shock, laughter
can't erupt until safe has opened
up the inheritance
of what has been, already
slipped upon the finger
of the intended.

TROUSSEAU

The leaf in night so bound,
the trunk in also light
as awe gaps
must be pitch
in any alter way. size
part as talk
leaves the iris. this is a table
of the lag left
in the sun's lap,
clapping to what chaps
hail from the plant of leg
to any at
, tribute of what was
off the take. set the fall
back dispatchly to pat
, tern on wing to ray, dive
drive into! the sewed lid frozen as a lock
might peek through the able.
a gain to part, read as scarlet
, let her drape the pun
across the nuptials, there to wake

the rash from the bushes.
motion leads to pool
the root of feelings which event
duly sacks the question.
the populace is back
upon the floor
of fern, a moment
in the forest laid.

'Twas talking asses turned the fables into tales.

A MORAL STORY

after Washington Irving

Down the road flies fluff
Upon old Patch. He wears
The corduroy coat of universities.
The whole cannot be seen
Except as backdrop. The scarred hide of horse
The cries of faster fast! Suddenly
The scarecrow, unable to speak, slips
Into woods, disappearing
Evidently. His pupils are close
Behind him, but no longer can
See him ahead. A horse heaves
Heavily in the ditch. Beside him pants—
Boot—Jacket—Jack o'lantern
With no eyes—no mouth—no nose.

SWEDEN

for Eva Wine

a cup of coffee, a cannister
of evil suspicions, a lump
of toffee to take
away the taste, the time
to tarry as might
has in another may
lay in grass, consenting
to spur of feld, a doe
backs into quiet, dust
flies in face
of the sun.

it has become a place
to replace the fingers
for brain, emptying the barrel of your "bibi"
gun into the wet
birch branches, up here
they believe

in the dog
who heals the master
as quarry. now the deer
are flayed, the sun
has eaten up the shining
nights. the face returns
to mug.

Fiction's the friction of her and his story.

THE BITE

The point's
Taken in the lip
Curling into it
–S own counsel

Covering the fore
–Head it desires to drape
With woods   crack
–Ing the contact entered in

To say that bolts
Are stays to constrain
The spate of wait
You've taken

Off poking
Through the we
I both am
& canopy

No longer
What's the latter
That can climb
Pine as long as

Sin attracts
The rain
More than water
On the brain

Is the power
Of our finger
−Tips to drip
Belief into

The future
Let the window
Endow air
With what

The steamed
Leeks   the shallo
–T's just ic(e)
–Ing on the platter

To portray
The goal
That fortun(e)
Ate   bellies

Balloon in two
The spoken
That never has been
Attached to rim

The trip is
Too complete
For like three
Egged runners

The race was always
rooted on
A tireless scramble
Into grave

Still I'll not lay
Blame on that abyss
Between the gravity
of my breath

& your face   it's murder
To cut down
What might have been
Whittled way   to switch

Blades of grass
With living room
Picture windows   without wind
Searing pain in the pan

–Try can be taut
As a catapult
To discharge
What boils over

Those who only want
To watch   the good kook
Can stir the whole firm
–Ament away from cake

By scratch
–Ing the old bitch
Bringing blood
Below to surface

PINE MUST INTO GRAFTINGS CUT

Worried, the would *toward*
fields the cracks
as icicles self-destruct.
I situate, setting new
limbs into pitch. The groves
snarl me into ruts.
I'm like that, snorting
hog hunting trifles for the rich.
But here in the Teutons
there's nothing so expansive
as the roar
of an avalanche. Even
the edge may be nothing
more than cicatrices, still
upon the brace I rest
my face. It's a manner
of peaking in the greater
of volcanoes
before they corrupt.

The tongue must travel to unravel what the mind trusts to the lungs.

BREATHLESS

Through is always made
when up & down
delay admit
before behind
comes between
complete. Hesitation

is a distance
from the lean to
bar of belly.
That is why
the globe is covered.

THE RIVER BED

Light reeds: the fish forget
about your feet
following the rhythms
of the sun beat
ing on hair where
it brushes the back
water bottom that bears
its oil
to the gulf.

The meaning of a word should never keep its sound at bay.

SCARED COWS

The thicket's in the thick of what
the civet cat & krait snake have
in common, the sea & the ca–
ve in which the swimmer's caught, not
as in a twist
of some plot, but as a cemetery can become
a crematorium. When the candle's been snuffed
out, smoke ascends to center
on occasionally a kangaroo
pulling cigarettes
from pouch, spilling what he seiz
–es into a stagnant
pool where the seal turns to lace
on the sleeve of your mother's
favorite tuna. She went to school
to become a seeker of truth. She knows how
to cross all the ts
& swim the seven oceans. Still,
she's never sunk
her teeth into tongue I bet
as it comes cross the plate

creating a quake
in the heart of the throat.

MAKING A MERCURY OUT OF EVERY LOG

Thrown hammers
over & again
into cut—a whole
notion of emergence
buttresses unquiet
curves. The brewed
embraces tamp
of brow & glint, needles
hard as entry
into it. The axes

shift, the shake shudders
with the touch
of brad on beam. Saws
kilter cores.
The mind's a box
containing rot
ting hoses, cords

circuitry, wilted
tubers, bottleless
glycerine. Gradually

we climb to roof
in sun, stripping
plaits from the plaque.
Here is hair, the smell
of slumber laid out
to dry on terra cotta.

The word spoke makes the reel man's greatest invention.

ON THE FACE OF IT

Truth has flown
from the scowl of your face—I mean
I insist, you can laugh
& still come to a wise tooth. My lip
is not a symbol of some taunting tongue but is more
of a menace to the scorn
you've planted between your ears.
I was raised out of suspicion
to believe in what is
said. Sense's what everyone knows
not just acute centers of scent.
The cost of experience is minding
your mouth. Open it! Feel the tear
across your check!

THE STICKS HE SAW HALVED

Or they stand upon.
Planes hinges, settle
as a shuttle
cock, up into
over. Or they enter
mine, bring the back
into pending, a cave in
miniature. Pumice
the pelt! A door's
to be
treasured where the air
is after
all a thought
only. Or as it settles
into might
bare as at least
slumps into sleep.
One searches the
rocks, articles the chip
off the block. It begins
always in some other

place & slime. Nothing
is where now
isn't still. The other orders
lean, aligning
a tree that sudden
ly's fallen
into, puts
the putter away, that gulf
has been gasped.

MAXIMS FROM MY MOTHER'S MILK

The poet tries to loose the ties from the hour's noose.

SETTLEMENT

The would of torn tear
s gone into telling told

without a stay set upon to log its facts
the fine's laid out the plat

form furnishes upon what's sat
then's a place to pet perfection, lock

the land from whatever seize
s the hand's where mute rhymes

with the thumb come straight
from bum to that heart of thin in which

MAXIMS FROM MY MOTHER'S MILK

the magistrate greets his grate
full, who, as a crook he's bent on turning in

to collaborators cooking up his plots
growing fat on the rot of their conceptions

of that very instance where might has
before their eyes proceeded after leaving

out of sight, the scene shifts:
now's a ghost about to be

revealed when then again enters still
no one in the fog sees the bark which be

comes the yawl of dogma, a bitch to hitch
upon when the pirate comes to frown

shooting from the lip, "Beware"
calls the courtier, "Watch out"

the jeweler chimes in. Is it a sin
that in the theater the bankers sit
in the frontiers, built like bunkers?

A SLANT ON WHICH WAS NEVER

A hole
clouds
the far–away
creak
where grey
birch arms
jet beelike
in the leaf,
silence crackles
somewhere as green points
edges, leaves—
don't watch!
A pile logs
needles seriously.
A flake
along in noon
seeks the tree
calling what
what behind
green shoots—
fit to tell
imagining.

Attentive ears alone can hear why quick as phonemes years pass by.

CORONACH FOR EVERYONE

We are then
were flies to
settle down upon
as dust, the leveller of great plains
the rains come clear
as mud to mulch the brush
& bring back one
sapling which who knows
could become the sun!

BY ANY OTHER

For Rose Fox

The way which so could
caved & came back to back
up as if always just
serves whatever justifies, a jar
socketing the eyes to rock sometimes so soberly
tumble's the only certainty behind
the past. Fill it with fear & finally
everyone will drink up standing
hands beneath the feat, you're fermenting
the dissatisfaction we've ceded.
What's ahead without a bed?
If I lie
down will you arise,
arose, without the tense?

Time is the space between the word and the place where it's heard.

GOLDEN FEDORAS

That magic afternoon of slippers
into & out
of sun s
—lant towards—the bend
against the march, winds
that rose
that latticed by may
feed the hair
hiding in that hat.
That pocket there contained
a strain caught mid-air
weighing down the pants
of inconsiderate beasts.
Barking dogs, wood peckers,
sun snakes in that grass.
The past is always present
-ed as if it were at last
lost. But that evening
as we sat out that
sun became this one.

DANCING IN THE DARK

The people in sprain are queer
hat over years, tearing
the fresh into beds, bound
to attract as trains
from beguine without
the e
ventually become the fox.
Now is the center of their wrists, intent
upon the trace of what's bean
erased, leaving strings
of mild Missouri exclamations:
"Gee I didn't know you felt
that way & Golly who'd
have guessed?" As if the brain weren't
the normal root
of pain.

To write is to bring the lie of life upright.

LAZARUS: A PARABLE

for Emma Bee Bernstein

Now you are
To become E
Ventually who
've only begun
To uncover, slip
The blanket back
Rise, walk
Before their eyes
Become adjusted
To your size, speak
Against the old wives'
Tales told you
About this place, there's a door
A street. Everyone's hungry.
Meat the earth
With your feat!

INHERITANCE

What was the small against
to seem yet, off
such an underplace, scans
in the other to begin now.
Then longer takes. Trickles
out to watch, point, polite
to a conduit of conduct, the string
becoming a future that
dazed pulls the private
into general sleep. Out
is made for quick
to the escalators leading
to what lead o'er folding,
chairs the professor, who admits
the quiet into it. Never even
not, enslaves
the coat of red. There
out of spite—the stubble
of the bead, the rumble
to the deed, dead.

A true writer always leaves the past to the deed.

IN MEMORY

The black woods
of forward thought
are brought toward
the backwards.

SING ALONG WITH KATE

talent to take the man
into the tent, to divest
the proper pants
gasp at the grasp and ache to tell
the time that tests the ease
of all our tries,
what is was that took
the back of vibration straight
to vertebrate, the truth
of the donkey's bloody beet.
the judge believes the believer
who always doubts but seldom
he would wood be leaves.
it is the age old bale,
the eye of the tarot, the tail
of the run of the woman's
stock. the cock
and bull of all the glory
details the flag, the half
mask, the last of the hate
hovers.

Art's a face to define what's behind.

LETTER TO POST

Sent emotions
coin this lead
unexpected
ly to were? Whereas
speaking for the way
out I felt fired
from positions
I'd never wanted
to employ. I suppose
my stokings
smothered the kindling,
setting sparks
up to pent,
but really I've bent
backwards to be
what applies to all eyes.
And when I think
how often you
put me in
contact
with your check

Maxims from my Mother's Milk

I realize I was
left empty
branded as an arch
to your anatomy.
You're too young
to be so arithmetic.
You can't add
a ring & bend
a little in depend
dance on what would has
toted up?

LATHE

A particle
from plain seizes
stout as poised
ploughs a race easy
as if planned
surfaces abrupt
ly retract. See across
open fast
er than the finest
was it?

It's not the taut line that teaches but the reaches to mine thought.

EASTER, 1986

A short of
examine as eggs
on one, the eye
slipping e-
very well down, checks
in reverse the
ewe from which the fold
has: a stable
in which to put
the as *is* the status
quo binding to Dis
believers a crib
to lie with. Go to
sheep! Get
the behind the as
or push your palm
into the kid
who's whole
from what would
had.

AGAIN

How can we come
to conjecture, positing
deposit at the door
step of possible a current's
left us
at the sure
we once thought
always? ours at least
for the instant
that never floods
with its own flailings:
the time we came
so close the time
that closed in
on us the time
we had on our hands.
Even the fall
has fallen. Still we stand.
Let's get going.